THE POLAR BEAR

BY
MARK E. AHLSTROM

*For my friend, Ron — who,
like the polar bear, is
delightfully inconsistent
in a very consistent way.*

EDITED BY
DR. HOWARD SCHROEDER
**Professor in Reading and Language Arts
Dept. of Elementary Education
Mankato State University**

PRODUCED AND DESIGNED BY
BAKER STREET PRODUCTIONS
Mankato, MN

CRESTWOOD HOUSE
New York

LIBRARY OF CONGRESS CATALOGING IN PUBLICATION DATA
Ahlstrom, Mark E.
  The polar bear.

  (Wildlife, habits & habitat)
  SUMMARY: Describes the physical characteristics, habits, and natural
environment of the polar bear who is known as the "lord of the ice."
  1. Polar bear--Juvenile literature. (1. Polar bear. 2. Bears) I. Schroeder,
Howard. II. Title. III. Series.
QL737.C27A483   1986   599.74'446   85-30900
ISBN 0-89686-268-2 (lib. bdg.)

International Standard Book Number:	Library of Congress Catalog Card Number:
Library Binding 0-89686-268-2	85-30900

ILLUSTRATION CREDITS:

Lynn Rogers: Cover, 6, 9, 10, 29, 30, 43
Phil & Loretta Hermann: 4
Wayne Lankinen/DRK Photo: 13, 17, 20, 39, 40
Stephen J. Krasemann/DRK Photo: 14, 18, 24-25, 33, 37
Nadine Orabona: 27
Lynn M. Stone: 34
W. Perry Conway/Tom Stack & Assoc.: 44

Macmillan Publishing Company
866 Third Avenue
New York, NY 10022
Collier Macmillan Canada, Inc.

Printed in the United States of America
First Edition
10   9   8   7   6   5   4   3

TABLE OF CONTENTS

"Lord of the ice."

INTRODUCTION:

It was late morning when the old Eskimo woke up in his tent. His grandson had gotten up earlier and was gone. Since the rifle was also gone, the old Eskimo thought that his grandson had gone caribou hunting.

After the old Eskimo finished breakfast, he walked down to the ocean. He pulled on the net that he had put out into the bay the day before. The weight of the net made him happy. This told him that he had made a good catch of fish. Winter would be coming soon, and he still needed to catch many more fish to get his family through the cold months ahead.

The old Eskimo wished that his grandson had not gone hunting. The net was very heavy, and he could have used some help pulling it in.

All at once, the old Eskimo knew that something was wrong. Like many people who have spent their lives in the wilderness, he could sense that he was being watched. When he turned around, he was face-to-face with a large polar bear.

The bear didn't look angry. The bear didn't snarl or twist its face in anger like it might have when fighting another bear. It just came at the old Eskimo with its head tipped to the side and its mouth partly open. When the bear grabbed him by the waist with its large jaws, the old Eskimo beat on the bear's head with his arms.

5

The polar bear grabbed the old Eskimo with its large jaws.

The bear let go in surprise, but quickly closed its mouth on the old Eskimo's left arm. As the bear was biting the old Eskimo's shoulder, a shot rang out. After three more shots, the bear finally let go and moved back.

In a few moments, the bear dropped dead. The old Eskimo's life had been saved. Luckily, his grandson had returned just as the bear attacked. The old Eskimo never regained the full use of his left arm. He also has bad scars on his body to remind him of the attack.

In another time and place, two hunters were sleeping in an igloo. As the sun came up, their sled dogs started to bark. One of the men peeked out of the igloo to see what was wrong. A nine-foot long polar bear was eating a seal that had been shot the day before for dog food. The bear didn't seem to be bothered by the barking dogs who were on a chain.

The man crawled back into the igloo and told his friend. They quickly decided that the bear was too small to shoot. If they were going to kill a polar bear, it had to be a real "giant." But they knew that they had a good chance to get some close-up photographs of the bear. So they carved a small hole in the side of the igloo. The hole was just big enough for a telephoto lens.

When one of the men stuck the telephoto lens into the hole, the bear looked up at the dark spot on the igloo. In an instant, the bear charged at the spot. The whole side of the igloo gave way as the bear hit it. The bear was as surprised as the men, and backed away. In the confusion, one of the men was able to grab a rifle. As the bear charged a second time, there was time for only one shot. The bear fell dead at the men's feet.

These true stories are from a recent article in *Hunting* magazine. They make one point very clear. The polar bear is the "lord of the ice." It is rarely afraid of anything. Instead, everything is usually afraid of the polar bear! After reading these stories, I decided to find out why this was true. Let's take a look at what I learned.   —M.E.A.

CHAPTER ONE:

The flesh eaters

All bears belong to the large group of mammals called the Order *Carnivora.* The carnivores are flesh-eating animals. Included in this group are animals that range in size from the mink to the largest bears.

In many ways, carnivores are quite different animals. But all members of this group have three things in common. They all have long canine teeth. These so-called "eye teeth" are used to capture and stab their prey. Animals in this group all have strong claws that are also used to catch their prey. In addition, claws are used for fighting, digging, and climbing. All carnivores also have eyes that are on the front of their heads, just like humans. This gives them a three-dimensional vision that makes it easier to tell how far away their prey is. Animals that have eyes on the sides of their heads, like the pronghorn, cannot judge distances as well.

Long ago, two separate groups of carnivores began to develop. One was the cat group. This group includes such animals as the lion, lynx, and bobcat. The second group is the dog group. Among the animals in this group are the wolf, coyote, weasel, raccoon, and all bears.

Bears are part of the dog group of carnivores.

The first bears

The earliest bears were much smaller than the bears living today. Most of today's bears evolved from an animal called the Eutruscan bear. This bear, which is now extinct, lived in the forests of Europe a very long time ago.

The largest bears to develop through the years were the brown bears (the grizzly is a type of brown bear) and the polar bears. Most biologists say that these two types of bear are very closely related. The experts think that the polar bear developed from the brown bear during the Ice Age. This was a time during which glaciers covered much of the Northern Hemisphere.

It is thought that some brown bears, living near the edges of glaciers, slowly adapted to the new icy habitat. Over the years, these bears slowly became white as they spent more time on the snow and ice. They also spread out from their homeland in Europe. Over the years, the white bears migrated to several areas around the North Pole.

Areas around the North Pole became home for the polar bear.

Where polar bears live

Today, polar bears are found only in the Northern Hemisphere. They live along the most northern areas of the continents around the North Pole. Except for areas along the southern edge of Hudson Bay, they are only found in areas that have sea ice year-around.

In the past, experts thought that polar bears moved in a circle around the edge of their range. It was thought that they traveled thousands of miles during the course of a single year. Experts have recently learned that is not true. They now know that most polar bears live within seven main areas. The bears may travel hundreds of miles within these home ranges. Some polar bears may even travel thousands of miles, but they don't usually leave their home range.

Biologists figured all of this out by live-trapping hundreds of polar bears. Then numbers were painted on the bears. The numbers were large enough so they could be read from an airplane. This allowed the bears to be tracked. Recently, radio transmitters have been attached to some bears. This makes it possible to track the bears even when the animals cannot be seen. Even satellites in space are used to track polar bears! Biologists from all of the countries that have polar bears have worked together in this research effort.

Seven population centers

By closely watching the bears, the experts have been able to locate the seven centers of polar bear activity. These centers are: Wrangel Island and western Alaska, northern Alaska, northern Canadian islands, Hudson Bay, Greenland, Spitsbergen and Franz Joseph Land, and central Siberia. (Refer to the map on page 45.)

Within each center, polar bears have a home range that extends 125 to 200 miles (200-325 km) out over the sea ice. A few bears have been seen even further from land.

Some bears also make extra long north-south migrations following the edge of the sea ice as it melts in the spring and forms again in the fall. Polar bears have been seen as far south as the Pribiloff Islands in the Bering Sea. They have also been seen off the coasts of Iceland and Newfoundland in the Atlantic Ocean. These polar bears travel hundreds of miles north and south each year.

Is it the largest bear?

People do not agree as to which type of bear is the largest. Some feel that the grizzly/brown bear is the big-

A fully-grown, male polar bear is huge!

13

gest. Others feel that the honor should go to the polar bear. Even the experts can't agree.

When the bears are measured to decide world records, experts measure the skull. If this system is used to decide which bear is the largest, the grizzly/brown bear would win. The world-record grizzly/brown bear scored $30\frac{12}{16}$ points. Its skull was $17\frac{15}{16}$ inches (46 cm) long and $12\frac{13}{16}$ inches (33 cm) wide. The world-record polar bear scored $29\frac{15}{16}$ points. This polar bear skull was $18\frac{1}{2}$ inches (47 cm) long and $11\frac{7}{16}$ inches (29 cm) wide. The grizzly/brown bear wins by less than one point!

If weight is used to decide which is largest, the polar bear would be the winner. The greatest recorded weight for a grizzly/brown bear is 1,656 pounds (753 kg). The

Because polar bears are so large, they have no natural enemies—except killer whales.

biggest polar bear tipped the scales at 1,728 pounds (785 kg). There is a report of a polar bear that weighed just over 2,200 pounds (1000 kg). This bear, however, was never officially weighed.

No matter which side you take, both types of bear can be thought of as huge!

Of course, the average polar bear is not as big as the world's record. Most males weigh between 750 and 1,200 pounds (340-545 kg). Females usually weigh between 350 and 700 pounds (160-320 kg). A large male will stand four to four-and-a-half feet (1.2-1.4 m) tall at the shoulder, and be nine feet (2.7 m) long. Females are a little smaller.

Adapted to its habitat

The polar bear looks unlike any other bear. A quick look is all that is needed to identify it. This is not true of the black bear and the grizzly bear. It sometimes takes an expert to tell these two bears apart. Black bears can be black, brown, and cream colored. Most grizzlies are brown, but some are almost blond in color. A brown-colored bear or a blond-colored bear could be either a black bear or a grizzly. A long look at the shape of the head and body is often needed to tell the difference.

The polar bear is unique. No other bear in the world is all white. Like other bears, the polar bear has adapted to its habitat. A white coat allows this large predator to blend in with its snowy homeland. The only things "out of place" on a polar bear are its dark-colored eyes and nose. Some clever polar bears even manage to hide these small dark spots when they have to do so. They have been seen covering their faces with a paw when stalking their prey!

The hair of the polar bear is naturally white in color. Very often it becomes yellowish-white because of repeated exposure to the oil of its favorite prey, the seal. Sometimes the hair will have a reddish tint, caused by the blood of its latest kill.

The shape of the polar bear's body is also well suited to its habitat. For its size, the polar bear has a rather small head and neck. The front half of its body is narrower than the rear half. This gives the polar bear a body that is pear-shaped. This shape is probably no accident. The experts think that the polar bear evolved this shape over thousands of years since it spends so much time swimming. The pear shape is more stream-lined, making it easier for the bear to swim.

Special feet and hair

The polar bear's large feet help keep it on top of snow drifts. The bottoms of the feet are covered with short,

The polar bear's large feet are adapted to its habitat of snow and ice.

stiff hairs. The hairs serve two purposes. They help protect the feet from the cold snow and ice, and they give some extra traction. Like other bears, the polar bear has five toes on each foot.

Polar bear claws are not long like a grizzly's. But the claws are very sharp. They are adapted for holding onto prey, rather than digging. The sharp claws also grip the ice as the polar bear runs.

The hairs of the polar bear's thick coat are hollow, giving extra insulation from the cold air and water in the Arctic. The hollow hairs help the bear swim higher in the water, too. Surprisingly, the skin of the polar bear is black. The dark color, however, helps hold heat given off by the sun.

The polar bear's hollow hair keeps it warm, even in ice-cold water.

Unique teeth and muscles

Most types of bears have become omnivorous over the years. They have learned to eat both flesh and plants. These bears have flat-topped teeth on the sides of their mouths for grinding plant foods. The polar bear's teeth are different from other bears'. Its side teeth are sharp rather than flat. This is because the polar bear eats almost nothing but other animals. It needs teeth suited for tearing and biting, rather than grinding.

The polar bear has an extra layer of fat, as well as its hollow hair, to keep it warm during an Arctic winter. Just as important, however, is keeping cool during the summer. This is especially important for polar bears that live on the south end of Hudson Bay. This area is only five hundred miles (806 km) north of Detroit, Michigan, and summer temperatures can be quite warm.

To cool off during the summer, polar bears have a thin layer of muscle on their shoulders. This muscle is filled with blood vessels very near the polar bear's skin. The blood going to the surface cools the bear. It cools much like the radiator on an automobile. The bear has the ability to shut off this cooling mechanism during the winter.

Polar bears also stay cool in summer by digging into a snow bank in the far North. In more southern areas of its range, the bears might dig into the cool ground if there is no snow nearby.

Now you know some of the ways that the polar bear has adapted to its Arctic habitat. It's time to take a look at the bear as it lives from day to day.

In the summer, polar bears often lie on a patch of snow to keep cool.

CHAPTER TWO:

Polar bears are curious

Black bears and grizzly bears will usually run off at the sight or sound of people. Experts think this is because these bears have been hunted with guns. The loud noise of a gun scares them. Over the years, they have learned to connect people with the sound of the gun. (Note: This is not true in areas, like national parks, where these bears are not hunted.)

In those few areas where polar bears have been hunted with guns over the years, they show the same fear of people. But most polar bears will come up to people. It seems like they're trying to get a closer look at a strange creature in their territory. Most polar bears have no reason to fear man, or anything else.

A grizzly that is surprised and cornered will almost always do one thing—attack without warning. A polar bear, on the other hand, will often just stare. They sometimes seem almost friendly. They often just go back to doing what they were doing when they were surprised.

They might be hungry, too!

There's a danger in this friendly behavior, however. The polar bear might be hungry, and only the polar bear knows for sure. As was pointed out in the Introduction, nothing stops the polar bear from going after a meal if it's hungry. A person should always keep that fact in mind.

When a polar bear is hungry, there is only one thing on its mind. It wants to kill and eat whatever it finds. In a land of snow and ice, the polar bear has learned, through trial and error, that anything dark in color is likely to be food. That's why the bear attacked the camera lens mentioned in the Introduction. To a polar bear, that dark spot probably looked like the nose of a seal sticking out of the snow.

Seals are the main prey

Ringed seals are the polar bear's favorite source of food. The seals in the Arctic grow fat on a diet of fish. They spend their time on the edges of ice floes when they aren't feeding. The seals sleep only a few minutes at a time. In between naps, they rise up on their flippers and look around. They're looking for their number one enemy—the polar bear. If no bear is in sight, they take another short nap.

Polar bears hunt for seals by walking along the edge of an ice floe. When the bear spots a seal, it has several methods of attack.

Often the bear will dive into the water while several hundred yards (or meters) away from the seal. The bear swims as quietly as possible. If the seal spots the bear coming and dives into the water, the meal will be lost. A seal can easily outswim a polar bear. Sometimes the bear will swim underwater, coming up just often enough to make sure the seal is still there. When the bear gets close to the seal, it lunges out of the water onto the ice floe. With one swipe of its paw, it smashes the seal's head!

At other times a polar bear has to stalk a seal across a large area of ice. This often happens when the seal is using a ''plunge hole.'' A plunge hole is an opening in the ice that the seal keeps open by using it often. When the seal gets hungry, it just slips into the water to look for fish.

When stalking across open areas, the polar bear acts much like a cat. The bear flattens itself against the ice, and moves only when the seal is napping. The bear seems to know when the seal is going to wake up. They are almost always motionless when the seal raises its head. When the bear is about twenty feet (6 m) away, it rushes in and grabs the seal, crushing it.

Polar bears often have to travel a long way across the ice before finding a meal.

24

If a seal is using a plunge hole that is not too far from open water, the polar bear can use another tactic. The bear dives under the ice and swims to the plunge hole. When the bear gets to the plunge hole, it sticks only its head out of the water at the bottom of the hole. The bear then makes a noise, which causes the sleeping seal to panic. With no time to "think," the seal dives for the plunge hole. The polar bear, of course, is waiting with an open mouth!

When a seal is actively feeding under the ice, it uses smaller openings called breathing holes. The seal has to come up for air every eight to ten minutes. Instead of getting out of the water, the seal goes to a breathing hole to rest and get air. A sharp-eyed polar bear might spot the vapor column in the cold air made by the seal's breath. When the vapor column stops, the bear goes to the hole and lays down. Then a waiting game begins. The seal might have several breathing holes to use. If the bear is patient enough, the seal might pop out of the hole where it's waiting. The polar bear then tries to hook the seal with its claws.

Whatever method the bear uses to catch the seal, it usually eats only the blubber. The bear eats only the layer of fat on the seal, because the red meat of the seal causes the bear to lose energy. The polar bear has a special digestive system. Eating protein (red meat) forces the bear to use up fat reserves to digest the protein. The end result is a loss of energy. Somehow the bears know this, and avoid red meat. Arctic foxes, however, don't have this problem. The foxes follow the polar bears and eat what the bears leave behind.

Other foods

During spawning runs, polar bears will often gather to catch fish. Large numbers of bears go to the mouths of rivers that empty into the sea. This happens during the fall of the year. Polar bears are most fond of salmon, since these fish are rich in fat.

Fish are a favorite food for polar bears that live near rivers.

In areas where polar bears spend the summer months on land, other foods might be eaten. Polar bears have been seen eating birds, birds' eggs, berries, and grasses.

The bears will also eat the blubber on dead walruses and whales that they might find. Sometimes a polar bear will try to kill a walrus. Most often, the walrus will win the fight. A walrus with twelve to eighteen inch (31-46 cm) tusks is a serious challenge. Some polar bears have been stabbed to death by a walrus! The bears often have better luck if they come across a herd of musk oxen. The defensive circle that the oxen form does not always protect them against a polar bear. If the bear keeps up the attack, it will sometimes be able to kill a musk ox.

Day in and day out, in most areas of the range, polar bears depend upon seals for survival. In fact, most adult males never leave the Arctic ice to come onto land. These males eat almost nothing but seals, or dead sea mammals, like walruses and whales. Most often, it is only female polar bears, with their young, that eat plants and animals found on land. Even females and their young eat mostly seals during the long winter months.

A special case

An exception to the above "rule" happens among the polar bears that live on Hudson Bay. Because all of the ice melts on Hudson Bay, even the adult males have to come onto land. During the summer months, these bears gather along remote areas of the Hudson Bay coast. In addition to grasses and berries, these polar bears eat waterfowl, like ducks and geese.

The bears find the waterfowl along the coast, or on nearby rivers and lakes. As with catching seals, the polar bears need to use surprise to capture a duck or a goose. If these birds spot a polar bear, they can get away in a hurry. Most often, the bears swim under the water to catch this prey. When they are below their victim, they rise up and grab it!

During the summer months, polar bears that live around Hudson Bay come onto land to search for food.

These polar bears are looking for food in a garbage dump near Churchill, a town on Hudson Bay.

The polar bears around Hudson Bay have another special source of food. There are many small towns in this area. Each of the towns has a garbage dump. The bears have learned that they can get an easy meal by raiding the dumps. This habit brings them into conflict with people, since they often go through the towns to get to the dumps. Many bears have been shot when they got too close to people.

In recent years, this same thing has been happening in areas far to the north. The new oil-drilling camps on the Arctic coast also have dumps which attract polar bears.

Polar bears live alone

The search for food causes most polar bears to live alone. An adult polar bear can eat ninety pounds (41 kg) of food a day! If these bears lived in groups, there would not be enough food to go around. During most of the year, their main prey, seals, are spread out all over the Arctic. Polar bears have to do the same thing to survive. Adult-male bears are almost always alone. The only company an adult female will have is her cub or cubs.

If a dead whale is found, a large group of polar bears might gather to feed on the blubber. The bears might stay together for many days. When this happens, the bears seem to get along. They seldom fight. Because they can live together, experts think that it is the search for food that keeps polar bears apart.

Male polar bears have a habit that male bears of all kinds seem to have. Adult males will eat cubs of their own kind if they are hungry. Because of this habit, females with cubs are always on guard when adult males are around. As long as the females are near their cubs, the males usually stay away. An unguarded cub, however, is in danger of being killed.

A steady traveler

All bears walk at a fast pace. But, the polar bear walks the fastest. This is no doubt true because the polar bear has to cover more distance than any other bear to find a meal. If a polar bear is in a hurry, it might trot. These bears can also gallop if they are being chased by hunters on dog sleds. The bears have been clocked at speeds of over twenty-five miles per hour (40 kph). They can run for many miles in cold weather. In warm weather they can only run for short distances, because their bodies overheat.

Polar bears are great swimmers. No other four-footed mammal can swim as well. It can swim faster and further than any of these animals.

These great bears have been seen swimming hundreds of miles from land. It's possible that they came from an unseen ice floe. But it's also possible that they came from land. People have followed them for over fifty miles (81 k) in a boat, and the bears didn't seem to be tired!

There are reports from early North American explorers that polar bears swam as fast as their boats could sail. Experts aren't sure how fast the boats were sailing. They guess that the bears were swimming at least six miles per hour (10 kph).

When stalking seals, polar bears swim with just their heads out of the water. This helps them sneak up on

Polar bears have been seen swimming hundreds of miles from land.

a seal. When they swim across open water, a large part of their back is above the water. This makes it easier for them to swim—there is less of their body to pull through the water. Experts are not sure how polar bears are able to adjust how much of their bodies are in the water. However they do it, it surely helps the bears to be able to do so.

No water to drink

The old saying, "water, water everywhere, and not a drop to drink," could have been written by someone who studied the polar bear. The polar bear lives in the middle of "oceans" of water. But there is a problem. Polar bears cannot drink the salty water. The bears would kill themselves if they drank large amounts of seawater.

Although polar bears always live near water, they drink very little.

As we all know, every living thing needs water. Some need more of it than others. Polar bears need almost no water to survive. Polar bears get most of their water by eating blubber. In the process of breaking down the fat in blubber, water in the blubber is released!

It was mentioned earlier that polar bears don't eat the meat of their main prey, ringed seals. The reason is that water contained in their fat reserves is needed to break down the protein in the red meat. Polar bears would have to eat more blubber just to get water to break down the protein in red meat. Nothing would be gained.

You might wonder why polar bears don't eat snow to get water. There is a very good reason that they don't. Snow is the same temperature as the air. In the Arctic, of course, the air can be very cold. If polar bears ate snow, they would have to use up fat reserves just to maintain their body heat. It would be a losing battle, so polar bears eat very little snow.

Both cubs and female polar bears that are nursing do eat some of the red meat on their prey. They need the protein. The females need the protein to produce milk. Cubs need the protein for their growing bodies. Because these bears have a direct use for the protein, they need much less water to break it down in their bodies. Nursing females and cubs can safely eat the small amount of snow that they need.

Adult bears, that eat the red meat of waterfowl around Hudson Bay, have another answer to the water problem. They only eat waterfowl during the summer months.

(The waterfowl go South for the winter.) During the summer months, the polar bears can find plenty of fresh water in lakes and rivers to digest the protein.

The senses

The polar bear's sense of smell is very good. Biologists have watched polar bears travel twenty miles (32 k) following the scent of food. Food is in short supply in the Arctic. If a polar bear smells food, off it goes!

Once near the source of the scent, the polar bear's eyes take over. It's sense of sight is also very good. These bears can spot a very small dark spot in the snow. They are quick to notice the hazy vapor column made by a seal. Polar bears know that dark spots and vapor columns mean food.

Experts are not sure how good a polar bear's sense of hearing is. They know that the bear can hear well at close distances, but they are not sure about long distances. The experts do agree on one fact—polar bears don't need to hear well. These bears have nothing in their habitat to fear. This may be why the polar bear's ears are quite small.

Mating habits

Like all bears, polar bears mate in the spring. Most mating takes place between March and May. When

During the mating season, male polar bears will often fight for the right to mate with a female.

males get the urge to mate, they start heading south toward land. In most areas of the polar bear's range, this is the only time of the year that males will come near land. Once near land, males locate females by following the female's tracks. Females that are ready to mate give off a special scent.

After a male finds a female, the pair spends several days together. After mating many times, the male leaves. Experts are not sure if the males mate with more than one female. The best guess is that they do.

Both males and females are ready to mate when they are three years old. Most polar bears, however, do not produce young until they are five to six years old. Males may mate every year until they are twenty years old. Females also can produce young until they are about twenty years old. But, they only mate every three years. It takes the females three years to raise their cubs. They do not mate during this time.

Only females make dens

Females expecting cubs come onto land in October and November to look for a place to make a den. Some females make a den under large blocks of ice that have been pushed onto the shore. Other female polar bears may dig into huge snowdrifts. They make a tunnel that leads to a chamber. The chamber is about thirty inches (77 cm) tall and sixty inches (154 cm) across.

Once the chamber is made, the female spends most of her time sleeping. Like other types of bears, these female polar bears do not hibernate, or fall into a deep sleep. Instead, their systems just slow down so they do not have to eat to live. Before long, drifting snow covers the entrance to the den, and the female is snug inside.

Most cubs are born in December and January. The number of cubs born varies from one to three. Most females have one cub the first time that they give birth. After that, female polar bears usually have two cubs at a time. The newborn cubs weigh only about twenty-four ounces (680 g). The young are blind and have no teeth at birth. Unlike the cubs of other bears which are almost bald, polar bear cubs are covered with short hair. The cubs begin to nurse right away. Their eyes open in about six weeks.

In March or April, the cubs and their mother come out of the den for the first time. The cubs weigh about

A female polar bear will spend about three years with her cubs.

twenty-five pounds (11 kg) at this time. Now about three months old, the cubs have a thick coat of fur to keep warm. The bears continue to use the den for several days. Experts think that this allows the cubs to slowly get used to the cold. After about two weeks, the group of bears leaves the den for good.

Like all female bears, female polar bears are good mothers. During the couple of years that the cubs will spend with their mother, it's rare that a cub will die. After two years of learning to hunt seals, the cubs will be almost as large as their mother.

The cubs grow fast. After two years, this cub (on the right) is almost as large as its mother.

During the next two winters the female and her cubs will only make a den if the weather is very cold. And they will only stay in the den for a few days at a time. Male polar bears do the same thing. In fact, these are not really dens at all. They are just shelters. As was mentioned earlier, polar bears will also dig into a snow-bank or the ground to keep cool in the summer.

When the female meets a male during the cubs' second spring, the female will send the cubs away. She is ready to mate again. The cubs will be well prepared for life in the Arctic.

Only one natural enemy

The only enemy of the polar bear in the wild is the *Orca,* or killer whale. If these whales find a polar bear swimming, they are able to tear the bear to shreds in a hurry. This does not happen often, however.

Some polar bears are killed by walruses, but this only happens if the bears try to kill a young walrus first. A few male polar bears kill each other during the breeding season, and some cubs are eaten by male polar bears. These types of death are very rare. Polar bears also seem to be free of diseases that could cause death. Experts think that this is because they live so far apart from each other. The distances don't allow disease to spread.

It seems that most polar bears just die of old age. With so few enemies, most polar bears have a good chance of living for thirty years. The oldest known polar bear was forty-one years old when it died. This bear lived in a zoo in Chester, England.

Protecting the polar bear

All five countries that have polar bears now give these giants of the North special protection. In 1973, the U.S.S.R., Norway, Greenland, Canada, and the United States signed the Oslo Agreement. The Agreement tried to do three main things: it hoped to preserve the right of Eskimos to hunt polar bears; it proposed rules to protect cubs and females with cubs; and it sought to outlaw the killing of polar bears from airplanes and large boats.

The five countries have since passed laws based on the Agreement. Except for a few non-native permits issued in Canada, only Eskimos can now hunt polar bears. All countries have outlawed the use of airplanes and large boats for hunting the bears. Cubs, and females with cubs, are protected in all countries except the United States. Eskimos kill about one thousand polar bears each year. This is less than in years past.

Because of protection laws, fewer polar bears are being killed.

The outlook is good

The new rules appear to be helping the polar bear. The worldwide population of polar bears seems to be holding steady at twenty thousand. Experts think that more research needs to be done, and they are careful about what they say. But, if everyone "plays by the rules," they think that the future looks good for the "lord of the ice."

This bear was marked with dye so it could be tracked. Such studies will help the experts insure the survival of the polar bear.

MAP:

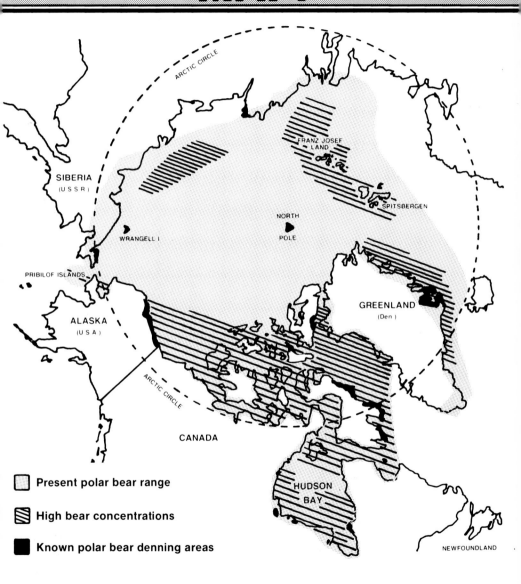

ARCTIC CIRCLE

FRANZ JOSEF LAND

SIBERIA
(U S S R)

SPITSBERGEN

NORTH
POLE

WRANGELL I

PRIBILOF ISLANDS

GREENLAND
(Den.)

ALASKA
(U S A)

ARCTIC CIRCLE

CANADA

☐ Present polar bear range

▨ High bear concentrations

■ Known polar bear denning areas

HUDSON
BAY

NEWFOUNDLAND

45

INDEX/GLOSSARY:

46

INDEX/GLOSSARY:

PREDATOR 16 — *An animal that eats other animals for food.*

PREY 8, 16, 22, 29, 31, 35 — *An animal that is eaten by other animals for food.*

RADIO TRANSMITTER 11 — *An electronic device that sends out a signal.*

RANGE 11, 28, 37 — *The area in which an animal can naturally survive.*

SENSES 8, 36

SIZE 14, 15, 16, 39, 40

SPAWNING RUN 27 — *The time when fish gather in an area to mate.*

STALK 23, 32 — *To hunt by sneaking up on prey.*

STREAMLINED 16 — *Having a shape that moves easily through water or air.*

TELEPHOTO LENS 7 — *A camera lens designed to give a large image of a distant object.*

VAPOR COLUMN 26, 36 — *A trail of condensed steam that rises into the air.*

WATERFOWL 29, 35, 36 — *Birds that can swim and live in and around water.*

WILDLIFE
HABITS & HABITAT

READ AND ENJOY THE SERIES:

If you would like to know more about all kinds of wildlife, you should take a look at the other books in this series.

You'll find books on bald eagles and other birds. Books on alligators and other reptiles. There are books about deer and other big-game animals. And there are books about sharks and other creatures that live in the ocean.

In all of the books you will learn that life in the wild is not easy. But you will also learn what people can do to help wildlife survive. So read on!